T0130560

THOUGHTS
of the
Confined
MiND

Perceptions within Reality

J L BOYD, SR

Trafford rev. 06/04/2020

North America & international
toll-free: 1 888 232 4444 (USA & Canada)
fax: 812 355 4082

Acknowledgements

I lost my mother first, and then my father. While they struggled most of their lives, they both did what they could to see to it that my siblings and I had enough. There is no doubt that the love from Olga Iris Gonzalez and Arthur Henry Boyd, Sr., was unconditional. I love you both, always. Peace and blessings be upon them.

Special thanks to Brandi N. Risen and Dometria Johnson, who are both dear friends. Without either of your support and undeniable love for me, I may not have survived through one of the toughest times in my growth and development. You both should have solidified your entrance through the Heavens gates for assisting in saving a wretch like me. Thank you.

Introduction

I would like to consider myself a revolutionist, though the truth is I've never actually stood up in revolt to anything of honest meaning. In fact, I haven't led anyone besides myself down a path less likely traveled. I'd rather claim to be optimistic. It's safe to say that throughout my life I've found the good in people and situations, taking into consideration that there are two sides to every story. Furthermore, through my personal experiences, negative energy only obstructs progression. It wouldn't be incorrect to credit my position on most topics to my upbringing and/or past. Having to endure much, without a doubt, made me stronger, wiser, amongst many other positive attributes, but it wasn't until I found my purpose that anything in life made any sense.

I was convinced that I knew exactly why I made the decision to write not only this book in general, but each piece of poetry itself, though it wasn't until after reading Alice Walkers, "In Search of Our Mothers' Garden," did I actually realize its purpose and the need for such literature. To possess a message is one thing, with delivering that message being another, but to have it heard and deciphered properly changes the purpose almost completely. A critics' focus is on criticizing, what in his opinion, is either irrelevant, non-factual, or so on and so forth, though nevertheless, his opinion. (Let us not misunderstand my perspective of critics; there are some who give constructive criticism. A skeptic may beg to differ, though the truth is at times we must accept reality and not certain facts that would only satisfy our own overview.)

To continue, if we were to label the job of the reader, you could say he/she were simply to read the material in search of whatever form of gratification intended. With that said, I feel that regardless of who purchases, criticizes, or passes up the opportunity to read this piece of literary work once in rotation, the books intentions will affect the nature of the environment as a whole due to the simple fact that someone somewhere will surely by captured by its true intendment.

To explain further, poetry, in my opinion, is much more than euphemisms, semantics, and even more than one's personal expressions. Poetry possesses life, meaning, and/or definition. In most cases the poet lives through the piece. To pass judgement on another's life would be to take claim of possessing god-like attributes, which would understandably be a stretch. If you feel the same way then I'll assume you're in tune with my point of view.

Thoughts of the Confined Mind

The Moon, The Sun & Qualms

Savor the bittersweet joy
    of justice
Poetic justice,
    as it may seem

As the shadow moves
    due to the constellations pendulum
    And its swaying,
    Timeless,
    Consistent motion

The frustration of futile,
    frivolous noise,
On occasion,
    swarms one mental state
Of mine
Mice
    And men...
In this case its not that simple
For simplicity is of the curious
    And while every button
    has its limit,
The higher self speaks of infinite

The mind is certainly the all,

The moon, the sun & qualms...

"The Confused"

Lost souls
Abandoned by society,
Found by lusts
    for a dream
Thoughts
Confined in the mind
Yet the eyes won't open,
    so belief is unseen

Curiosity dwells in a dormant state,
Afraid of reality
A relaxed sacrifice
    of failure
Breeds fictional agreements of oneself
And such actions are repetitive...

- Based on the youth, in a world which lacks significant leaders -

"Land of Lost"

Life essentials:
    A heart,
        A beat
    A mind and a though
Free will
    leaves the responsibility of choice
    to the chooser
"As a result, their minds became dark
    and confused
        Claiming to be wise,
           they instead become utter fools"[1]
Only after learning the lesson
    can you teach,
The blind,
    therefore,
        can not lead the blind
Nor can the deaf
    hear the message.
Tangled in the chains of vanity,
    Pride
    Self-satisfaction
And "If truth becomes for us a value worthy of
suffering and risk, then we shall overcome
fear – the direct reason for our enslavement."[2]
The goal of the lost
Is to be found
        [1]Romans 1:22, [2]Jerzy Popielustzko

"Caged Bird"

Ever watched a bird enjoy free space?

Consumed by the air which surrounds him
A flawless sight
Solace in the clouds
Altered by the sun

As motion moves
So does time
Paving the sky for the moon

And as he continues to allow
      The scents,
      The sounds,
      The breeze,
To motivate his wings
He remains
      speechless
           for he hasn't a voice

Only free space

"Death Threats"

Threatening Thoughts

Why live if you haven't a life?
Clock ticks while caged away,
Cast away like an anchor

A lock with no key
Sitting still without a dream
Fist clenched
            to fight a thief
The stolen gifts found
            in hates possession

Oh, but contrary to beliefs,
And though deterred,
            no suicide will be witnessed
I won't kill time,
I will murder hatred,

I can't sleep

Yes,
            I can dream/succeed

" Why Lie"

You said you'd make me a winner,
You told me to believe in a lust
Unfortunate was I in the end
     since left alone to make amends
     with my self

You lied

Said I feel alive
Told me you were the answer,
When I only had more questions

Late nights lacking sleep
     nor did I dream
Deferred
     Caught up by death threats!

"Kill 'em"

Kill 'em
Kill 'em dead!
He stole a dream!
A hard fought battle,
Lost to greed,
So kill 'em,
     Kill 'em dead!

Broken promises
Loves mischief
Ignorance,
Stupidity's the blame, rather

"Suicidal Thoughts"

Curious mind of mine,
      Why do you choose to fight?
I wonder if you expect to win
      And what exactly
            or do you even care?

Such a vindictive one!

Lie,
      Then lie some more
      Forcing to an action
While blind to the hurt you cause
You leave me to suffer!

Think your right
      When your so wrong,
So argumentative
And its repetitive

      But I'll get you!

"Quotes"

Nothing
      Comes to a sleeper
      But a dream,
      Though awake
      (while) in the dream,
      Bring life
            to the thought
            once you Rise!

Curious mind of mine,
Why so negative?
Hatred roams,
      violence fueled by past
      mishaps

Battles of the conscience
Constant
No rest,
      fatigue

You should chill,
      Be still (focus)
And produce growth!

"Love Letters"

3 Words

You and I
I and you,
Could have lasted
Without an effect
Without an effort
Nothings there forever
Simple sudden change
Tears of pain
Anguish though love
Always and forever!

"Sobeit"

I hurt for a pain
      Because I can't feel
I don't understand the
      meaning
Tortured by a scar
A wound from a mistake
      that healed nevertheless
Sobeit!

"Selfish Message"

Pardon the interpretation,
Could things be truly at ends?

Never mind the sincerity,
Prosper,
Keep your heart close to your shoes,
Love takes you on a slippery journey,
Wouldn't want you to fall!!

"The Guitarist"

The language is the music,
        as the musician plays

The scene,
        A pale stone colored backdrop
                in tinted attire

While the sun reflects off each cord
The fingertips' speech,
        Well spoken,
        Speaks volumes to such a still
                address

Blind to any vision
To words,
        deaf

Aimlessly playing
Beautiful, aimless playing
One could imagine the rhythm
        to which he plays
such rhythmic play

Just listen…

"*Synonymous for Time*"

Less like a frolic
More like a subtle jog
Fruitless without efforts
  and attention to what's beneath the fog
Luxurious in its beautiful frame,
Curious once or twice,
  as to the exact purpose,
  its aim
Not once but twice,
  passing by,
Yet the opportunity is due
Like a butterfly when he first flies
To whom the stars align
The moon and sun will rise
  And rise
  And rise
Never seeming to enthused about their fall

"Times Death"

Feathers on a caucus
Imagined by the day dreamer
Stilled by the time
Wasted in a sense
Spent pondering the future
While forcing the present

Murderer!

"Sing Song"

Sing Song
Mama Died
Daddy Gone
Son Cried
      Daughter the same

Sing Song
Still Alive
Restless
Can't Win
      For Losing

Sing song

Intermission

I feel like I've lived long enough to truly believe that no matter what, life goes on. I hear that regardless of what I may face, there is always someone who has to endure much more. Well I say, though this may very well possibly be true, their struggles are their own. Perception does matter, but will not affect the physical conditions. Furthermore his/her issues neither will lessen my pain nor change my situation, and of course vice versa.

I understand that none of us are perfect. Mistakes are a part of life, and every offense has a certain cause and effect. It would be easy to self-destruct or give in to the corruption called unforgiveness, and allow depression to take over your life. Forgiving yourself and others is indeed easier said than done, but the same energy and effort it would take to continue in a destructive pattern could also be used to elevate and rise above your transgressions. Flaws only makes an individual unique, because each of us are creations of our Creator, who Himself is flawless. While we may make mistakes, we are not mistakes. Our most unwarranted mishap is our sometimes inability to take advantage of the many chances given to us.

I believe we're ultimately judged based on our intentions. Leaving the judging to my Divine Judge, I'd rather not consider my past actions as either good or bad. Although, I can say that the majority of the decisions I've made along the way were done so with decent intent. I never hurt anyone intentionally who hadn't made a serious attempt to injure myself or a loved one.

And while some may feel there isn't such a thing as justifiable retaliation, I would have them tell that to my cousin who was stabbed 7 times almost losing his leg in an altercation; or to my sister-in-law who was shot for just being at home at the so-called wrong time; or maybe they'd have an easier time getting such a message through to the brother of a former friend of mine who was shot multiple times and killed outside a convenient store after attempting to diffuse an argument which took place when the club ended.

The fact remains that sometimes bad things happen to good people. Many different factors play a role in each situations outcome. If the perceptions of the aggressor hadn't been what it was then the retaliation would not exist. Recognizing the initial actions helps to understand the reactions.

Would it be farfetched to feel that while there is but one world, we as individuals live in separate realities? Ones not so much based on class, race, gender, or creed, but perception. How we see life is what gives life its essence. For example: I've been incarcerated. I was locked away from my child, family and friends. Everything I had was taken from me during that time away. After so long I was actually alone with just my thoughts.

For a moment you may feel sympathetic, to say the least, but I would have to ask why? Regardless of the crime committed or the reasons behind them, which would surely by justified if explained, though for these purposes will not be necessary, crimes are punishable by incarceration. The point here is that being alone with my thoughts is where I found my purpose. Solitude allowed me to look inside myself. I overanalyzed my past, paid close attention to my present, ultimately leading to much needed focus on my future.

A positive mind can only produce similar fruits. The same goes for a heart that has found purpose. Every individual possesses the ability to heal the mental wounds of their own and in some cases others. Possessing such strengths and refusing to acknowledge them only hinders one's own progression. We must give in in order to receive, an old statement that has been consistently true. The giving in this case gives reference to your effort. If you're reading this material then it's obvious that change is possible. Potential lies dormant in us all, and whatever the cause for its release, what a blessing it is.

"The Eyes Never Lie"

-We as outsiders only see what we can, but every individual has an inner struggle. It's only after a deeper look into a persons eyes that we truly acknowledge the hearts' pain...

Can you see 'em?
The brown skinned brother,
With his swagger, and that look in his eyes
Oh, those eyes!

Can you see 'em?
To the living, life is question
For him it seems the answer
Everything is a smile, never a frown
        And still there's those eyes
Covered with some sort of glass that only
        shows a reflection

Those eyes
The step, appearance and aura indeed only
        intensifies and compliments each element
        almost forcing a simple glance,
                Head to toe,
                Toe to head,
                        Only to meet those eyes!

Can you see 'em?
Wait, one thing comes to mind,
Not conceited, no, maybe self-confident,
Yes
But is this envy or hatred that's on the inside?
What's in his mind?

Can I see it?
No, but the ease in which he strides,
    that smile, the subtle tone he selects
    and effortless confidence when voicing
    his words

The words and those eyes mustn't have a care in the world,
I've seen him with his little girl
Should I wish to be him?
    Or one in the same?
Could I survive in his shoes for just a day?
Would I like to be able to stand what is unseen
    because now I realize something at a
    closer look into those eyes

Can you see 'em?
In fact I can!
Such pain, distrust,
A hardened soul from death,
    Maybe within,
No just his past, people close I can tell
And there's hurt from failure or just
    thoughts of failing

But damn!

Here comes that gloss,
Now recognized as held back tears,
Nevertheless a mirror,
A cover,
A door closed to hide those eyes
Can I really see 'em?
Yes
    Though its simply a reflection!

-I understand my life is a mystery to the unseen, the spectator's eyes. Blessed with many gifts that can be witnessed, and cursed with knowing what's inside. Before you envy or judge another, take a strong look at your own life because theirs is more than likely a simple reflection. We all struggle.

"Soldier?"

I'm a soldier because I fight for what is
      deserved,
Not because I fight
I'm a soldier because I'm at war,
      there's a conflict to be settled,
Not because I've been to war,
Though I'm in the middle of one at this moment
One within, one against right and wrong,
      not with men
Just a man is how I stand,

Come again?!

I've walked the road that's considered rough
      to most, and I'm living so I survived!
Been thru hell but how else could I recognize
      Heaven the very instant I arrive!

You say it is I who brought my life upon
      myself?
It is I, in fact, and that same individual isn't
      making excuses for his self!
And contrary to most beliefs, I will make it,
      one way or the other
Nothing's here to hole me back
With the heart of Malcolm X
And the will of Langston Hughes,
Not to mention, I'M A SOLDIER!

"Can't"

Can't never could
Can't is a sorry excuse,
A reason to not do what you could if you
     simply put your mind to use

Anything is possible
It only takes an effort,
Sitting around fussing about an issue
     is effortless

Can't means not,
And haven't you been told to many times
     what you couldn't?
When you could if you wanted!

So therefore you can!

Just do it!

You're the only person who "CAN" stop you!

Your only objectives, have-to's,
Is to live and die,
     which of course will happen,
You "can't" and won't live forever!

"*Time (Destination Unknown)*"

Is time really on my side?
I ask because it seems as if I'm captured in
        a web that holds me in a spot for
        a small time frame and only time will
        tell if in fact time is really on my side!

So high off of life!

Planted seeds and the end result is this:
A crash course on the societies constant
        impact on the urban street corner
It's not bliss!
But ignorance isn't the reason for such
        downfalls,
Maybe yours

Obstacles set us all back a bit, though no bid
        can stop a God given gift!

Present,
Tot eh strength of Rosa,
The hope of Martin,
The courage of Harriet, moving though
        the struggles with the unused
        power/ potential of Powell!

So either way, if time is or isn't on my side
        it's definitely all I have!

"A Man Cries" (Part 1)

-They say a man isn't supposed to cry. They say it is out of character, shows weakness, when in fact tears can be a sign of strength. Tears represent a lot, from happiness to sadness, and a man, every man, has feelings...

Look inside the sanguine eyes of a man
I mean deep down,
Where his respect lies,
Where his defenses looks to be losing
     its battle
Because his wife, girl or significant other
     continues to lie, cheat and steal,
     when all he's ever done is support,
     love and care for her
Never once has he raised his hand,
So his opinion hasn't been heard
Only around for the child
His past taught him about child support
Each check,
Each forward step sets him back
All without shedding a tear!

Look inside the troubled soul of a man
I mean deep down,
Where the pain lies,
Where he's unsure of how he is to support
     his family,
Raise his daughter,
And keep focused
All while separated by a wall
Where every movement is controlled

Told when,
Where,
And how
Where his thoughts are of no value
Yet he still isn't allowed to cry!

Now look inside that mans heart
I mean deep down,
Where it all begins and ends,
Where his will, love and strength lies
There's where you'll find how he still continues
      to survive through not just an average struggle
Through the prejudices of life,
All with a smile and his head held high,
Where his beliefs of a brighter day persists
      to be the reason he allows himself to get
      through that particular day
And that,
Only that,
Is in fact the cause for the tears that
      have been falling since the beginning!

"*Concrete*"

Rough,
Hard!
To hard to see or hear a heartbeat,
Though very much alive
Changes with the weather
Warm in the summer,
  as patrols patrol
Cold in the winter,
  keeping the block froze
When it rains,
It gets wet
Drenched in red
Echoes from the sirens bounce off,
  as they approach only to find the dead
Better known as the bricks,
Yet and still concrete
Home to many,
The house of few
The trash binder to crack valves, gun shells,
  Just about anything used
The homeless, the hookers, the hustlers too!
All of which are outlived by the bricks,
The concrete that is!

Part 1

"*Life*"

-There's power in words, even those that are written. From small phrases to sentences, each individual noun and verb are influential. Listen to the expression in these lyrics...

I hold dearly the memories from the past
Helps me hold my head in sights of the future
Looking to prosper,
And only proper preparation prevents poor
      performances
So when negativity arises
The sky is
Where my eyes face
Hoping to get wet
     Let the blessings rain down!
     Let the bells ring loud!
     Let the Heavens know that an angel
        has been born!
The truth set him free
The truth that only he himself holds the keys
     to be freed
Freed from a confined mind,
     Or should I sat torn?
Despised by the many who fell and falling
     to the devils reign
The devil is real, but does not reign
Over anything
That concerns this life!

It has been a war,
And so far
I've won most of the battles
But today starts,
With a morning that will tell if I actually grew
      mentally and have the smarts to overcome
      situations tougher than I've already
      triumphed
I simply have to take it in parts
One decision at a time
The God of my understanding is believing,
And I believe Him

Listen to my expressions!

Part 2

"Life"

Defeated and imprisoned
Pain stricken,
In search of revenge
Wizened up,
Smartened up,
Not a tear nor fear,
Just a smile
At the sight of a new beginning

Educated on a every level,
Instincts strengthened
Mental in tact also
Heart still pumping the blood of courage,
Bravery
Fulfillment of destiny
Predestined to win,
Without a quivering bone within

Steps without a stutter,
Speech spoken intelligently with no caution
Thoughts often
Flow like a river or
      Damn!

Pause for a breath, taken because this air
      has been loosened!

They understand what should have been
        understood
We struggle through mistakes but that
        doesn't define a man
Criminals are created
All crimes aren't heinous,
But those that are, should be punished

Punishment it is,
Not rehabilitation
Penalized because the past,
And such acts affect the present,
Let alone the future

So if a past is a past,
Can the present be a present?
A gift to the valiant,
Whose efforts were relentless
Wounds forgiven,
Since sutures have been given

By whom?

The Almighty Deliverer of deliverance
With His help, oh what future we could have
One where we smile at what we've
        accomplished
Established
On to a life which lives off love,
Lived until its finished
But never forgotten!

"Facts of Life"

Life itself is hard
Struggling to live
Each of us go thru a trial that could determine
    If we survive or die
Keep this in mind
    Your never alone
Your not the only one whose bills are due tomorrow,
    when you get paid the day after
And afterwards you still really don't have enough
    And Peter knows about Paul
It also costs for a U-haul
So your out in the cold after all
    is said and done
Keep your head up!
And you faith in the sky!
Because as time passes by
That female or male you trusted in
    still will cheat and lie
They'll still continue to deny
What's so blatant
Disrespect?
Spending their check to satisfy the next
Clothes, cars, jewelry and an expensive phone
    to hide an expensive text
Expensive because it catches them in the act
But still they choose not to accept
    the fact that their caught
And their wrong
Your not alone!
Call a friend
But only to find out its their number on your
    companions phone!

Aint life a bitch?
Well depending on how you dress her
Short skirts attract a certain kind of actor
Actor?
Acting as if his interests are in more
          though lesser
Messed up?
Prejudged
As it were in court when the judge handed out a
          sentence for dribbling nothing on tape
Your performance was limited
But look at your affiliates
Big rims and candy paint
I know it's stereotypical
But that's life!
Can only continue living it!
The strong survive, though the meek shall inherit
          the earth

From a forced birth to an unwanted death
Breathe deep but not to deep
This air isn't that fresh
Tobacco companies,
          Well lets not go there
          TRUTHWhadafxup.com
Continuously tries to communicate its knowledge
But who listens?
Blame it on rap music
Who are only musicians,
Artist trying to live and share their views on their neighborhood
and their life's struggles
And they continually misinterpret it
So whose fault is this?

Most homes aren't parentless
Rappers make up maybe 5% of the population,
    so if this kids' only source of profanity
We definitely live in a society where the media is
    the hegemony!
A media frenzy related to poverty ridden communities
Overshadowed by what's at a distance
Oil thief's
Causes more memorial reefs
    than N.Y.C.
    in 100° weather
Tension severed because colors not the matter
When blood spills
Sending chills,
But keep cool,
This is life!

-Untitled-

Good things come to those who wait
I've been waiting, and if you're suggesting
        I have so much bad, when that
        finally ceases, I'm to consider that good

I'm not a believer of luck,
Nor am I ignorant to the focal point of
        poverty
And it bothers me
Racism is stronger than ever
Contentment is the reason for the blind eye
        of such a naked deceiver
Consider that luck!

It's been said the less you know
        the less you'll hurt
Then there's the contradictory statement
        Stating that ignorance isn't bliss
So I'll ask you what's underneath your shirt?
I ask because you've been killing me
        slow and softly
With your offers
Offering nothing more than less
For loyalty,
While wanting me
To still respect myself
Huh!

Respect for myself is all I have,
When I've been stripped of all I had
And respect is the gift that continues to give,
Giving you real, raw, rather...

34

Wait!

I should give what I receive,
So this third finger from either side is what
      You'll get from me
Nothing more, nothing less,
Not another breath!

After Thought

The good in some of us finds itself encompassed by the walls of self. "The only devil from which man must be redeemed is self, the lower self. If man would find his devil he must look within; his name is self. If man would find his savior he must look within..."

At times we face trials that may raise certain questions of doubt: "Will I make it?" "Why is this happening to me?" And/or "How did I get myself into this?" Such doubt can hold an individual back, keep them from exerting the natural strength they already obtain to overcome their situations.

Our life accomplishments unfolds the necessary lessons to survive those trials to come. I'm sure the majority would agree that everything happens for a reason. And if this is the case, regrets should be a non-factor, encouragement moreso.

Most conditions faced throughout life aren't new except possibly to the individual. One way to look at any particular situations outcome is that there may not be a right or wrong way, but the best way. A person can only do what they are capable of, while the rest is left up to divine intervention. Experience is the best teacher, and with that said, hardships should be welcomed.

Living itself is only as difficult as you allow it to become. Of course there are certain occurrences in which we have no control, but we do possess the knowledge, understanding and wisdom to determine their effects on us. In my opinion, emotions are a consistent deterrent. As I mentioned earlier, fear and/or doubt will almost always hinder, if not completely diminish, a dream or goal.

During the course of life we trip, we fall, we overcome and then we repeat this process as we grow into the men/women we are to become. This simple thought of pain, not living up to ones expectations, can cripple the very idea of success. The thrill doesn't lie with the actual success, its in the struggle along the way.

The feeling that comes when your right at your climax. The very moment you exhale, lay back and smile. For some it becomes an addiction. They are those you may know moguls. I say mogul in its true definition; a very rich and powerful person.

When we think about power, we often limit this to the amount of money one has, though it's more related to the degree of control they have over another's mind. They say you get the money, then the power, and lastly the respect. Consider these all as rewards to your efforts. And please note that the money, power and respect we talk about in this instance does indeed come only to those who are rich. Rich in promise, rich in love, rich in hope, rich in patience, rich in charity.... On the right side of it all, is the drive, like a throttle. Each gear increasing the levels; the levels of satisfaction, as you undergo the more severe levels of suffering.

To many before me have already stated their position on materialistic thinking. Such assets as the cars, clothes, jewelry and large accounts depreciate with age. Though lets not be naïve, possessing those types of worldly goods will without a

doubt increase the width of a smile. Surely it is safe to say finances make the world go around. We'd all like to believe in love, music maybe, or whatever motivates an individual throughout their pursuit of happiness. But the facts are backed by statistics. A great man once said, "Men lie. Women lie, the numbers don't."

If all this is regarded as being true, then it is nothing more than a secondary blessing of the deserving; the fulfillment of their purpose being the primary goal of life. Very few people know their true objective. The search for what matters most in life is what should manipulate the earth's axis.

Each of us all has to look within to find what it is we were meant for. We're all optimistic in our quest for happiness, but without a clear path such a destination will look out of reach. When this becomes the center of attention, self-confidence weakens and we tend to give up on ourselves.

The greater part of the world doesn't realize the capabilities of the mind. This directly affects the scale of poverty, uneducated youth, teen pregnancy, and more significantly the death rate amongst other afflictions. All of which, frankly, influences the reproduction of society.

Ignorance is not bliss, and with knowledge being infinite, so goes the ability of the individual. To many times we lie to or make excuses for ourselves. This form of deception is the worst kind. If you're not honest with yourself, it enables you to allow anyone else to be close enough to even consider trusting them. Such actions aren't justifiable. The obvious explanation would include placing the blame on something foreign, when the quarrel is with self.

We as a civilization, in all honesty, are competent enough to recognize the necessities of genuine living. It is only when we are faced with a devastating event that we unite and put our minds forth towards a resolution. No one individual is perfect, but if each one reaches one, a starting point can be approached.

A mind on a mission has a vast amount of strength, with extraordinary capabilities. At times our mental capacity is used to store to much negativity. This leads to excuses, a direct interference of forward progress. One of the greatest poets, and forerunner of the Harlem Renaissance, Langston Hughes, asked the question, "What happens to a dream deferred?" Well thats one left for the curious minds of the many. Personally, I believe for few it lays quiescent while confidence increases, for some it may reform as a part of another path. And for others it diminishes along with their will to carry out what their Creator has set forth for them.

Every objective to be accomplished is first the product of a thought, though it is only by action that we acquire the benefits. Consider viewing your intuition as foresight. If your mind has the ability to see what's to come, then it would be safe to say it also possesses the power to alter its destination. And make no mistake; no finite mind can comprehend things infinite.

Think of a mans ideal as being his God. As he matures within his understanding, he then becomes knowledgeable of what love, truth, peace, freedom and justice is all about. Love, truth, peace, freedom and justice are the five highest attributes known to man. (Prudence combines them all, using them as tools for perfecting man.)

I could go on for pages, but to summarize life; we live and we learn. It all revolves around the mind. Wisdom is basically applied knowledge, and a wise individual not only knows better, but they show so with their actions. Common sense tells you when you've arrive at a decision unsuitable for the situation. One should practice making the proper choices by getting their heart and mind aligned. And it doesn't stop there, next objective should be placing those thoughts into action. Be patient.

Remembering that living with regrets is practically mandatory to move forward, will keep fear at ease. Proper preparation prevents poor performances! A statement that should always keep the mind focused. Stay determined and love yourself no matter what you put yourself through. In the end it will be that same love which will pick you up when you fall.

-"A life perfect aint perfect if you don't know
What the struggles for. Falling down aint falling
Down if you don't cry when you hit the floor.
It's called the past 'cause I'm getting past and I
Aint nothing like I was before..."-

Peace and blessings be upon us all.

JB The Poet

-I am willing to acknowledge… there are certain realities I must face about my life.

It is amazing, the stories we tell to avoid facing the realities in which we live. People drink, for medical reasons. Abused women say they fell down stairs. Abused and battered children needed the discipline. Rather than face what is going on, we will sit in the middle of a mess and call it a garden. We ride our boats down the river of denial and refuse to acknowledge the stench in the river. Even when the stench becomes unbearable, we say it is a good place to fish! We seem to have a really hard dime calling things what they are, which is probably why we spend so much time in bad situations. The longer we resist facing whatever it is, the easier it is to forget that we are equipped to change it.

The Bible offers us a story about a man who sat at the gate of the city begging for coins. When two of Jesus' disciples passed him without dropping anything into his cup, he asked, "Why?" The beggar explained his situation. He pleaded with the disciples for help. They refused! The disciples refused to believe his story because they knew the truth.

Instead of seeing the man as a beggar, they saw his power, his strength, his inherent right to stop begging and claim his Divine inheritance. They knew he was in denial. The disciples knew that the man called himself a beggar for so long he now believed it. The disciples refused to help their brother hold on to his limited ideas and beliefs about himself.

Wouldn't it be wonderful if you could stop buying into your stories and face the truth?

Until today, you may have been avoiding, denying, resisting the truth. You may have forgotten that you can do anything you choose to! You can have the kind of life you desire. Just for today, stop telling stories. Put the begging up away! Look at yourself. Look at your life. Tell the truth about what you see.-

Will you allow your thoughts to be confined to your mind?

J L Boyd, Sr. was born August 30, 1982. Raised in Harlem's Manhattanville Projects, until old enough to appreciate the differences in right and wrong. Boyd's bi-racial background is credited for his increased sense of pride, self-respect, self-esteem, and self-appreciation; all are key to ones personal growth and development.

Boyd survived several years of incarceration to walk the stage with an Associate's degree in Business Administration (SKYCTC), followed by his Bachelor's in Communication (University of Louisville). All while dedicating his life to uplifting the community through numerous events, speaking engagements and much more.

Printed in the United States
By Bookmasters